THE ART OF

LANDSCAPE PAINTING

Oils/Water color/Casein/Polymer

A
GRUMBACHER
LIBRARY
BOOK

INTRODUCTION

Landscape painting offers the artist a wide range of subject matter and an abundance of challenges. This is an area that appeals to the beginner as much as to the expert. To find an ever increasing measure of success and satisfaction, both the beginner and the advanced student need fundamental information on materials, composition, and techniques.

In this book, men who know how to paint landscapes and how to analyze them, graphically describe everything from ground work to finishing touches.

Here is your guide to the materials that will serve you best for a modest investment, and exciting direction that will make your creative time productive and satisfying.

Rather than devote space in the text to explaining terms, we include here a brief glossary for quick reference.

CHROMA: The saturation or purity of a color. Color intensity.

FIXATIVE: A colorless coating used to spray on drawings to prevent smearing. It can be applied by mouth atomizer or is also available in pressurized cans. (Myston)

GLAZE: Color thinned to a transparent state and applied over previously painted areas to modify the original color. (See also Underpainting)

GOUACHE: (Tempera) Opaque watercolors and the technique of painting with such colors using white to make tints.

HIGHLIGHT: The spot or spots on a painting or drawing on which light is the brightest.

HUE: A particular variety of color.

IMPASTO: A manner of painting in which the paint is laid on thickly so that texture stands out in relief.

MEDIUM: The material used for a drawing or painting, also the solution used to make paints more fluid.

UNDERPAINTING: Preliminary painting used as a base for subsequent glazes, or a textured base for subsequent painting not possible by direct application of color. (See glaze)

VALUE: Relative lightness and darkness. The relation of one part of a picture to another with respect to lightness and darkness.

WASH: Color or pigment in thin solution.

Designed and edited by Walter Brooks

Copyright © 1965 by M. Grumbacher, Inc.

460 W. 34 Street, New York, N.Y.

Library of Congress Catalog Card Number: 65-15431

Produced by Artists and Writers Press, Inc.

Printed in U.S.A. by Western Printing and Lithographing Co.

Oils are by far the easiest for the beginning painter to start with and for that reason we have devoted the major portion of our book to this medium.

Brushes are many and varied. The bulk of painting in oil is done with bristle brushes, and it is best for the beginner to stay with these. Sables (soft hair brushes) are excellent painting tools but when not properly used, or overused, they have a tendency to make your work slick or fussy.

Turpentine is generally mixed with linseed oil rather than used alone as a painting medium. Grumtine is an improved paint thinner which may be substituted for turpentine. Too much thinner produces color which may have a tendency to dust off when dry. A popular medium is ½ turpentine and ½ linseed oil.

The various artists represented in this book discuss colors in addition to those on the following basic list. You will want to add some of these colors as you progress. The following basic list of material and palette of color, however, can be used for a great variety of painting.

MATERIALS

COLORS: Cadmium Yellow, Light
      Yellow Ochre   Burnt Sienna
      Cadmium Orange   French Ultramarine Blue
      Cadmium Red, Light Thalo® Blue
      Alizarin Crimson   Viridian
      English Red, Light   Superba White

BRUSHES: (The brush style is designated by a letter following the series number.)
      F = Flats (long bristle hair) #2 #6 #10
      B = Brights (short bristle hair) #4 #8
      R = Rounds (pointed bristle brush) #6
      L = Longs (long hair sable) #10
      Sable (round) #4
      Filberts, long hair (oval flat) #4 #8

CANVAS: Can be purchased either in panels, stretched on frames, or by the yard for you to stretch.

PALETTE: Wood, plastic, or disposable paper palette.

PALETTE KNIFE: For scraping palette clean and mixing color.

OIL CUP: A double oil cup clips to the palette—one cup for the medium, the other for brush cleaner.

TURPENTINE (or Grumtine): For cleaning equipment and thinning medium.

LINSEED OIL: A medium to use with colors.

CHARCOAL: Either pencils or sticks for your preliminary sketching on canvas.

FIXATIVE SPRAY: For fixing the charcoal drawing on the canvas before painting. (Available in spray cans or for use with atomizer to be applied by blowing.)

PAINT BOX: A desirable piece of equipment for storing brushes, paint, palette and accessories, and for painting outdoors.

EASEL: A support for the canvas during painting. The lid is designed to act as an easel in some paint boxes.

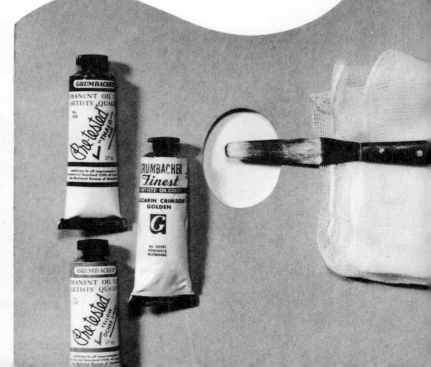

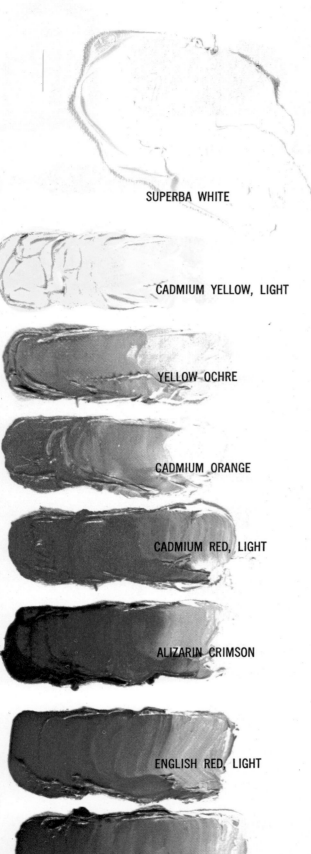

SUPERBA WHITE

THALO BLUE

FRENCH ULTRAMARINE BLUE

THALO GREEN

CADMIUM YELLOW, LIGHT

YELLOW OCHRE

CADMIUM ORANGE

CADMIUM RED, LIGHT

ALIZARIN CRIMSON

ENGLISH RED, LIGHT

BURNT SIENNA

Christopher Davis introduces the reader to a basic palette of oil colors and to the fundamentals of landscape painting.

Get to know your colors by brushing them out on your canvas to see the exact hues. Reduce each with medium to examine it as a wash. Add white to each and study the hues as opaque color. Learn the great variety of color possibilities that exist not only with all the colors readily available but within a limited palette as well. Try various mixtures—experiment.

It is better for the student to stay with the basic palette of ten colors plus white until he is thoroughly familiar with them. The palette can be increased as facility improves.

As an example of what can be obtained from a limited palette, the sketches on the opposite page were painted with the colors shown next to them. While it is true that some subjects lend themselves to a limited palette more readily than others, it is better to learn to work within a limitation and increase the palette gradually than to flounder with too many colors at the beginning.

Note the range of greens possible by the addition of white and intermixing from the combination of the three colors shown.

These three colors with various mixtures of white make possible a wide range of beautiful grays.

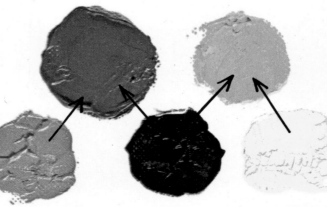

YELLOW OCHRE · THALO BLUE · CADMIUM YELLOW, LIGHT · YELLOW OCHRE · THALO BLUE

CADMIUM ORANGE

THALO BLUE

FRENCH ULTRAMARINE BLUE

BURNT SIENNA

CADMIUM YELLOW, LIGHT

ALIZARIN CRIMSON

THALO BLUE

WILLOW

APPLE

PINE

MAPLE

LAUREL

ELM

CEDAR

An important element of the landscape is the tree, either by itself or as part of the overall composition. *The importance of the basic silhouette, whether in drawing or painting, cannot be over emphasized.* If it is correct, your statement of the tree is well on its way. It is a simple matter to indicate depth of form by the addition of light areas and additional dark accents. Practice drawing or painting the simple contour shapes.

When painting, mass in the general over all shape with a brush and work your pattern of dark and light with a palette or painting knife for a textural quality appropriate to that of most foliage. As your facility increases, study the great variety of textures in different species and develop your personal approach to the indication of such textures as directly as possible without getting fussy or labored in the painting.

While it is not necessary to draw the skeleton of the tree in each case, you should have a feeling for, and understanding of, the structure and growth. This is necessary for proper placing of branches in the mass of foliage as well as indicating the basic silhouette to begin with.

Depth is created by the interplay of light and shadow.

Add variety by studying the patterns created by light against dark.

Study the pattern created by the direction of light. Mass the foliage by means of color of middle value; then add darks and lights.

Keep distant bushes massed and simple.

Note the spread at the base; trees do not go into the ground like sticks.

Foreground branches and foliage are dark; distance is suggested by lighter background areas.

Clouds that shift suddenly can be indicated directly and quickly with a palette or painting knife. Watch the overall shapes. Study the variety of types—edges hard, soft, wispy, stormy.

In approaching the landscape don't worry about minor details at the beginning. They can be filled in later if the painting seems to demand it. After the composition has been sketched in, look for the overall effect and paint it as directly as possible with brush or knife.

After sketching out your composition and completing basic lay-ins of color, try different ways of indicating the textures of various subjects. Half close your eyes and look for the broadest pattern of dark and light.

Mass distant trees; indicate form of trunks simply, either with knife, by scraping out, or with small brush.

The texture and color in a rock mass can be very exciting. Capturing the effect in paint is an interesting challenge. Work out the pattern of the darks; then with the knife or brush, work into this dark mass with slightly lighter browns, blues, etc. Now apply your colors of lighter value and work the desired texture into the wet paint.

For a delicate warm gray, mix Yellow Ochre, Cobalt Violet, and white. The shadow in the cloud should be on the warm side. Look for the great color variety to be found in clouds. In this case the finger was used to blend edges quickly.

The painting knife is an excellent tool not only for laying in color, but also for drawing into wet color to indicate textures, as with this old tree trunk, and for simple indication of tall grass. The knife also keeps one from getting too fussy with detail in the early stages.

The greatest difficulty for the beginning painter is the handling of trees and greenery in the summer landscape. For this demonstration Albert Pucci has selected a subject with a large grouping of trees; the building is of secondary interest.

A number of detailed sketches of trees and interesting shrubs were made with a felt pen and water color Lamp Black. (For this you could also use ink washes.) From this first viewpoint several compositions were made moving trees around where necessary. Then other sketches were made from other positions to vary the viewpoint. Black and white oil color sketches can be made on inexpensive canvas grained papers available in pad form. With oil sketches the palette or painting knife is an excellent tool for quick indications of foliage; the brush is used later for detail.

Try to achieve as much value contrast as possible. Note the different values of greens—some trees appear lighter in color and value than others. While making these black and white sketches jot down the names of mixtures of color that you might use in painting. This helps you to remember the impression of the subject that most interested you.

1. Once you are satisfied with your composition, decide what color and what value of that color will be most dominant in the overall painting. In this demonstration olive green of a middle value was most dominant. Start with Green Earth, Raw Umber, and Permanent Green, Light with a touch of Cadmium Yellow, Light. Using a large painting knife apply all colors freely and directly to the canvas, mixing on the canvas to achieve a fresh vibrant underpainting. Leave the application quite impasto.

When the underpainting is sufficiently dry, sketch your subject on it with a round sable brush dipped in Ivory Black thinned with turpentine.

2. When the drawing is finished, start laying in your lighter colors—the sky (a mixture of Thalo Blue and Superba White with French Ultramarine Blue and white) and sunlight on the trees and ground (Cadmium Yellow, Light, Permanent Green, Light, Cadmium Orange) all with white and intermixed in different degrees for each variety shown. Remember to permit as much of the underpainting to come through as possible.

By dragging your palette knife or brush over the surface of the underpainting you hit the high points, leaving paint on them with the green underpainting coming through. This gives an exciting textural quality and vibrancy to your painting.

Draw with the side of the knife as well as the tip or flat portion. The flexible blade, can be used to apply paint in an infinite variety of lines and textures.

Color on a bristle brush was drawn across the tree horizontally after the trunk was indicated vertically with a palette knife.

The textural effects shown on page 14 were achieved solely by the use of a palette knife and a flat bristle brush. Before starting to paint the following snow scene, I prepared the entire canvas with an overall tone of middle gray or gray blue (white and French Ultramarine Blue with a touch of Burnt Sienna). Then with the palette knife I proceeded to put in patterns of snow, trees, etc. This page shows three different compositions. Again, in all three sketches the first step was to prepare the entire surface with an overall tone. The snow pattern was put in directly with the painting knife, as were the buildings and trees against this middle value of color.

Look for the whitest white and compare this to shadow tones or the medium light tones. Shadows are never too dark on snow-covered fields. Shadows are darker in late afternoon with a strong setting sun.

In addition to the painting knife or palette knife, vary the manner in which the brush is used, and experiment with other materials as well. Try a sponge, cloth, paper, or anything that might seem appropriate for applying paint and creating exciting textures.

An interesting technique for these accidental effects is the pressing technique. This consists of applying paint in an almost creamy consistency, then pressing a piece of scrap drawing paper against it. The texture left on the canvas by the paper taking off some of the wet paint is extremely interesting. It is very good for the texture to be found in terrain. With practice you will develop control. After an area dries you can go over it and add more texture. A very good manner for treating large areas to keep them interesting.

1

1. Prepare canvas with an overall tone, as in the sketch stage previously discussed. This should be of middle value, usually a bluish gray (a mixture of French Ultramarine Blue, Burnt Sienna and white) or Cerulean Blue, Cobalt Blue, a little French Ultramarine Blue, enough white and a bit of Ivory Black. In this case mix on the palette but not too thoroughly. This underpainting should be allowed to dry sufficiently to permit you to draw your subject on it.

Sketch in the composition with a brush dipped in a thinned-out cobalt blue (see step 1).

2. Start to apply snow patterns with a palette knife. Some of your sketch will be obliterated as you do this but enough will remain to show location of subjects. Always be conscious of drawing as well as painting. One cannot exist without the other. Should you accidentally paint out areas already solved, don't panic! It is easy enough to recover the area by scraping off with the knife and restoring detail with a brush. Leave detail of trees and foreground till last.

3. Develop the dark masses of the buildings and tree trunk in the foreground. This is a combination of many colors in the finished painting, but is started with Burnt Sienna, Thalo Blue, and a touch of Alizarin Crimson mixed with a little white. The yellower browns of the buildings are a mixture of Burnt Sienna and Yellow Ochre with a touch of Thalo Green, again with white.

The problem of the snow should be solved first, obviously, because it would be impossible to paint it between branches.

Look over your painting—correct shapes, push darks darker if necessary, add more white with knife to trees, roof tops, etc.

Put the painting aside for a few days, then come back to it. You may see things to change—either color or tones. Be daring and free.

2

3

The following demonstration by Christopher Davis introduces an interesting approach that utilizes a fast-drying under painting to permit almost immediate over-painting with oils.

There is no subject area richer in pattern and texture for the landscape painter than the boatyard and waterfront.

In the jumble usually characteristic of such scenes, it is important to learn to be selective. By half closing your eyes and squinting you will eliminate the bulk of minor detail and see only the essential pattern. This observation and drawing will develop a personal sense of picture arrangement, which is one of the most important parts of painting.

The camera is a useful tool for recording detail, but snapshots themselves are rather meaningless when reviewed some months later unless they are accompanied by sketches to remind you of what originally interested you in the subject. Gathering material by sketching has the added value of recreating a much clearer visual image for you of the subject's mood, color, and effect.

The drawing to the right is a felt-pen rough (done to size of the final painting) for composition and arrangement of the color demonstration on the following pages.

The subject was painted on pressed wood prepared with Hyplar® Gesso. This gesso, an excellent ground for oil, can be used to surface canvas, plywood, pressed wood, cardboard, or any other non-oil surface. The colors were Hyplar polymer for underpainting and oils for finish. It is better to plan your painting only up to a certain point. Allow for the exciting things that can happen as you develop the various areas.

The oil color palette used was Zinc White, Cadmium Yellow, Light, Yellow Ochre, Thalo Blue, Viridian, Burnt Sienna, Alizarin Crimson, and Cobalt Violet.

1. The entire surface is covered with a middle value warm blue (Thalo Blue and Grumbacher Purple) and the drawing sketched in Mars Black. Polymer is used because it is so fast drying and makes an excellent base for the oil.

2. The color areas of the overpainting are executed in oil with the painting knife, scraping and rescraping to build up desired textures. Small areas are applied with either a smaller knife or brush.

As the color is put in a certain amount of drawing as well as texture is established by scraping it out again, as is illustrated by the water area. The texture and masses in the sky and various color areas of the boat were finally developed by a combination of glazing (putting thin washes of color over areas that have dried to subdue or accent them) and scumbling (applying a dryer pigment—almost as it comes from the tube—so that it brushes off on the surface letting underpainting come through).

In the following demonstration Dean Ellis, a distinguished painter and illustrator, describes another interesting approach, starting with a deep ground color rather than the middle value ground or the laying in of color areas on the white of the canvas.

Generally speaking the most successful subjects for an artist are those with which he or she is most familiar. This familiarity, the result of observation and drawing, comes through in the final painting as well as in the initial drawing with an authority that can be obtained in no other way.

A combination of many such drawings has become the painting in the following demonstration—and by re-emphasis and re-arrangement can become the source for many additional paintings.

Distant objects light, foreground dark.

Don't hesitate to experiment with value arrangements of the subject matter as shown here.

Lights in distance, sky and foreground dark.

Light from an unidentified unexplained source above creates a mood of mystery and increases interest in subject . . . foreground light.

1. This painting was executed over a previously prepared canvas painted with a mixture of Ivory Black and Cobalt Blue. After the ground was dry, the principal elements and masses were roughly indicated with light pastel and the painting was begun.

2. The sky, a mixture of Cobalt Blue and Superba White with a touch of Burnt Sienna to gray it, was laid in with a palette knife, and this surface was alternately scraped down and repainted to allow the texture of the canvas to come through.

3. Next the principal light masses were put down with a palette knife, but not as light as I ultimately intended them to be. The same was done with the darks, keeping them lighter than they would eventually be. In other words, at this stage the values were less contrasting than I intended them to be when the painting was finished. For the foreground a mixture of Yellow Ochre and white was used. The greens are Chromium Oxide Green with Yellow Ochre and white.

When the previous stage was thoroughly dry, broad glazes were brushed into the rock mass and foreground as well as over the light strip of building on the horizon.

After this the light areas were again worked on, this time with heavier paint and lighter values. Considerable attention was paid to edges where light areas met dark. Finally, details were added with small brushes and the edge of the painting knife.

Final touches and accents of the lightest lights and darkest darks were put down, these last at the extremes of the value scale within the tonality of the painting.

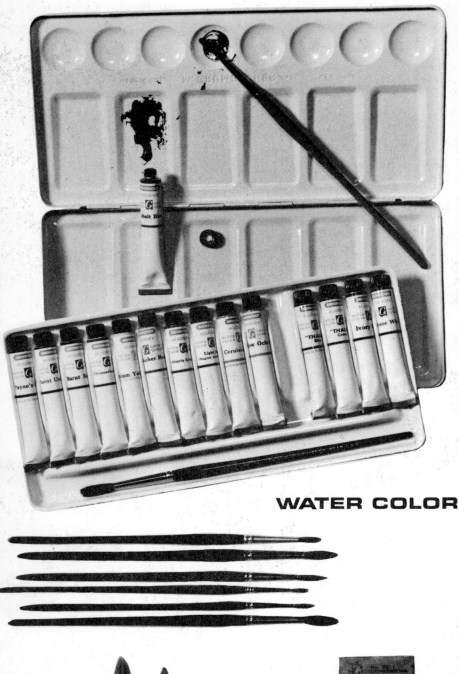

WATER COLOR

Clark Hulings, noted American painter and illustrator whose work appears in many public and private collections, demonstrates the technique of painting landscapes in water color.

The advantage of water color as a medium is that it requires much less equipment than does oil for location painting. Its drawback is that reworking has a tendency to destroy water color's most desirable quality—freshness and directness.

Water color demands great facility in brush handling. The "tricks," as they are sometimes called, depend not only on handling the brush but on the paper surface and many other tools such as blotters, sponges, razors, and masking materials.

Materials for Water Color

For your early attempts a good student grade set, like the one shown, should serve you well. You should select high-quality paper and brushes, however, if you wish to obtain reasonably good results right away. Buy the best brushes your budget permits, even if you have to start with just a few.

Paper comes in a variety of surfaces and weights. The principal types are hot-pressed paper (HP), which has a very smooth finish; cold-pressed (CP), which has a slight texture; and rough finish (R), which has the most texture. In the rough finish papers, there are many interesting surfaces and textures available. Heavier papers (140 lb. and up) are generally most desirable because they buckle the least when wet. There is a wide range of water color paper available in block, pad and sheet form. Water color paper also comes mounted on cardboard in the hot-pressed, cold-pressed, rough finishes. Recommended brushes are pointed sable brushes in sizes 3 and 12, flat soft hair brushes in the style called single stroke (here the ox hair variety should be adequate) in half-inch and one-inch sizes or the Aquarelle brush shown for putting in large washes and broad strokes. A sponge, blotting paper, pencils, and either a large plate, tray, or a mixing palette such as comes with the illustrated set are also required.

Your list of colors can be similar to those you used for oil painting. If you are starting with water color, however, your basic palette should include Alizarin Crimson; Cadmium Red, Light; Cadmium Yellow, Pale; Light Red (English Red); Yellow Ochre; Burnt Sienna; Burnt Umber; French Ultramarine Blue; Thalo Blue; Thalo Green; and Ivory Black. This list can be supplemented later with additional colors as desired.

As you become more experienced with the medium you will develop a personal palette of favorite colors for treatment of your subjects.

Keep statements simple and direct, as with trees. It is better to be fresh than completely accurate.

Dampen exact area to be washed in. This will help to control edges of color.

Draw figure over early wash; let it show through. Don't worry about mistakes or little accidents. Let whites of paper break through for sparkle.

Work from light to dark; remember, washes are transparent.

Wash allowed to dry before lines of roof are drawn in with smaller brush.

Since water color painting is a technique that develops more from experience—"tricks," if you like—than most others, the quickest way to get some facility is to throw yourself into it, make mistakes, slop around to your heart's content.

Assuming that you have had some experience with drawing and the approach to a subject, after five minutes of experimenting with the medium you will know what happens when you put color on a wet surface; when you blot your dry or half-dry paint, and that the color gets thinner as you add more water.

Cadmium Red, Light

Cadmium Orange

Alizarin Crimson

Sepia

Thalo Red Rose

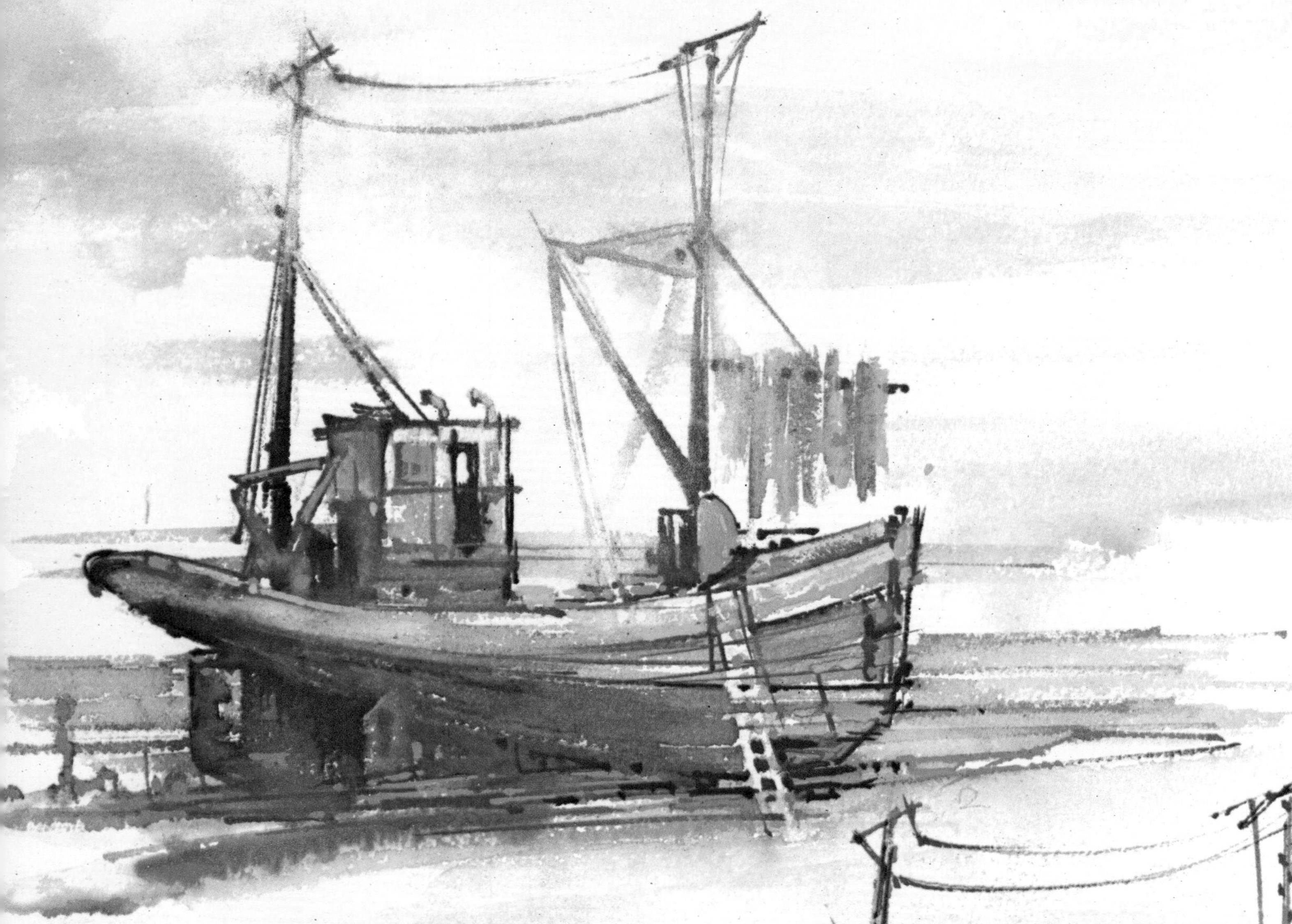

Here are two examples of the interest that can be achieved with a limited palette. Note how the subject need not be limited to the color immediately apparent but can be adapted to the mood or overall color effect of your painting.

It is best when starting with water color, to limit your palette. Add to your range of colors as you get to understand what can be done with five or six. The same subject is shown here twice, first in a range of reds and yellows and then in a range of blues and greens.

Thalo Green

Ivory Black

Cerulean Blue

French Ultramarine Blue

Chromium Oxide Green

Thalo Blue

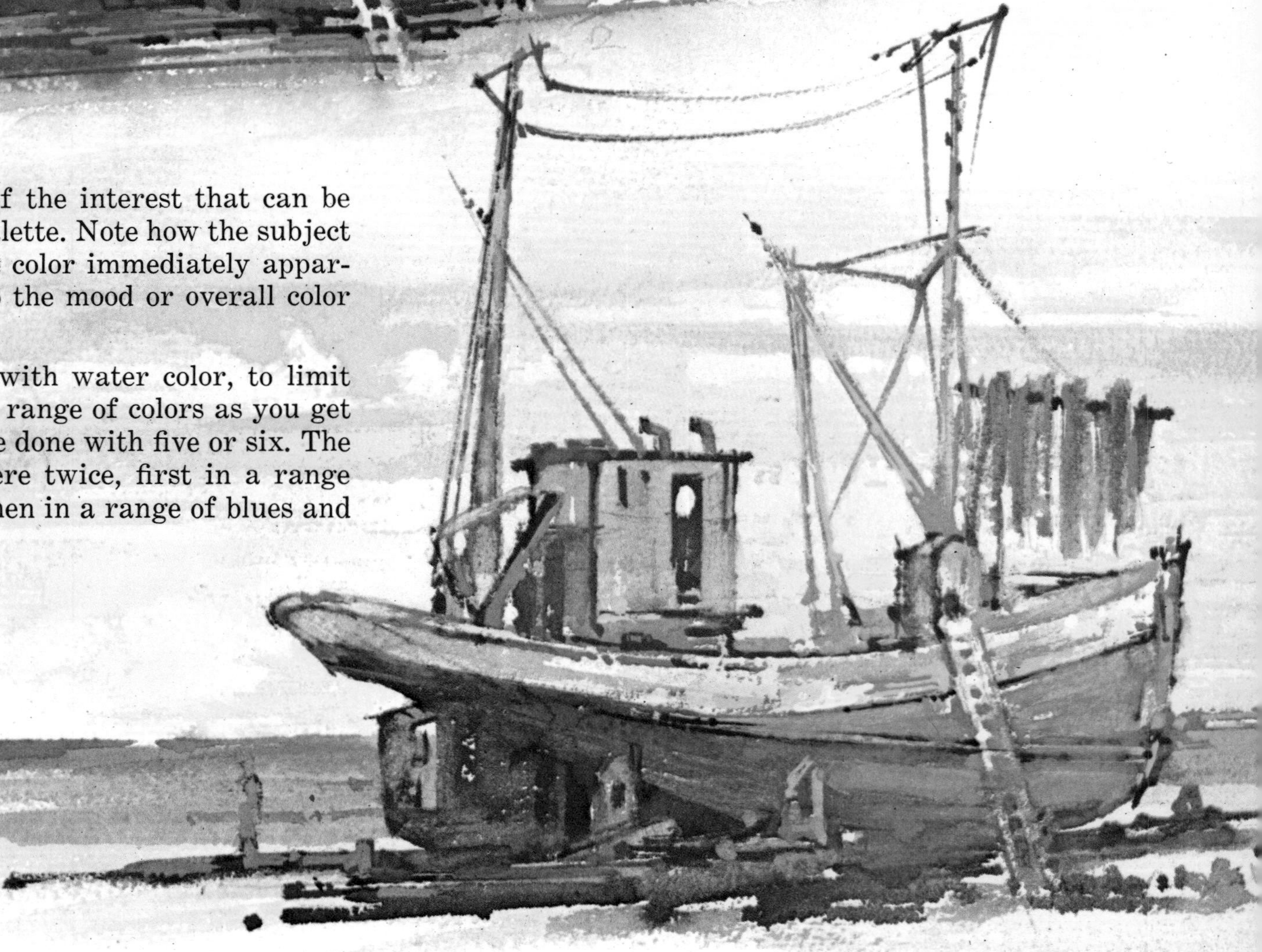

These thumbnail sketches demonstrate how a soft, homogeneous color effect can be achieved. The colors must be used sparingly and delicately.

1. After the paper was wet, thin warm washes of Cadmium Orange, Chromium Oxide Green, and Cadmium Yellow, Pale were applied to form clouds in the upper left corner, with subtle tints of orange and yellow in other areas.

2. A delicate wash of Alizarin Crimson forms the distant mountain and Chromium Oxide Green subdued with Sepia is painted over the nearby hill and horizon.

The painting is developed working from light to dark, using washes of Sepia, Alizarin Crimson, and Payne's Gray. These colors are washed in appropriately to form houses, piers, and beach line.

Water color is a medium of happy, *controlled* "accidents." A good water colorist makes these "accidents" work for him. He creates a situation where they can take place and he recognizes a desirable effect when he sees it and *leaves it alone.*

Some of the unique characteristics of water color which give it its looseness and charm are transparency, fluid washes, quick drying, and crispness (permitting sharp edges and fine lines). To feel at home with water color one should study these traits. The best way to start is simply by doodling. This experimentation can be real fun and shouldn't be inhibited by considerations of drawing, proportion, or any realism at the beginning. On these pages are reproduced a few such doodles with notes. Materials used were a number 8 pointed brush, a 9 x 12 inch Aquarelle water color block (140 lb.), a tube of Ivory Black water color, and a jar of water.

A wash of water—still wet, lines painted through it.

Heavy wash blotted with blotting paper. While still wet darker tones are drawn into it.

Brush loaded with pigment—little water (dry brush effect).

Lines painted—a wash of water brushed over them while still partially wet.

Blots suggesting foliage with lines put in after blots were dry—to suggest branches.

Brush loaded with water—little pigment (wet effect).

Heavy wash put down, vertical lines made by edge of blotting paper.

Varying density strokes suggesting fence. (The more distant the object, the lighter the tone for objects of similar texture.)

Lines of three density washes applied without permitting drying (see painting of trees on following page).

Scumbling of brush (dragging color across surface of paper by brushing with side of brush rather than tip).

Spatter effect produced by slapping brush loaded with pigment across the finger.

Tree—started with blots of medium wash with sky holes left white. Wet paper was held vertically and darker tone was applied above holes to indicate shadow under foliage. Darker lines were painted in after paper was dry. Grass suggested with splayed brush (by squeezing heel of brush to spread hairs, or brushing out on blotter until almost dry).

Wet brush blotted onto paper (side of brush pressed against paper). Sometimes useful for painting tree foliage.

One need not travel to find subject matter that will produce interesting, attractive, and satisfying water color painting. Look around your area of city or country; picturesque elements can be found almost anywhere. The unifying element in this particular scene is the effect of sunlight. To capture this, Cadmium Yellow Pale was washed over white paper to give every color subsequently applied a warm yellow cast.

A lavender of Thalo Blue and Alizarin Crimson was washed over the sky—kept as flat as possible. The lavender over yellow produces a warm neutral tone that contributes to the effect of sunshine better than a cold blue. By working colors over a yellow tone such as this a certain amount of vibrancy is produced that would not be possible if the same colors were mixed on the palette. Notice the variance in tone of yellow in the sky, the bits of yellow around the edges of the clouds, and the yellow tone showing through on the ground and in the shadow side of the shack. All this produces not only a vibrant effect but also gives a unity to the picture.

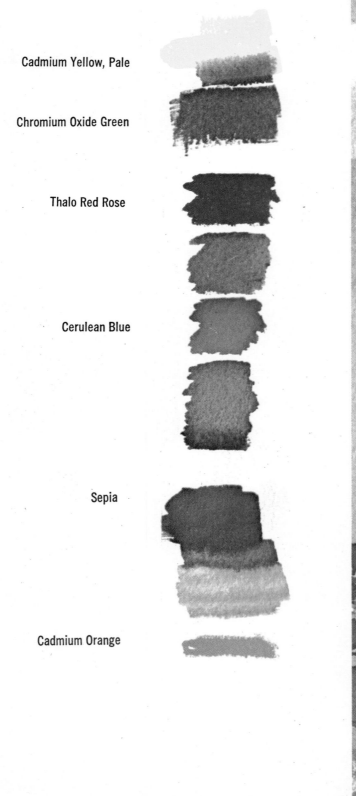

Cadmium Yellow, Pale

Chromium Oxide Green

Thalo Red Rose

Cerulean Blue

Sepia

Cadmium Orange

The shadow area of the building is painted an even tone, with color variations of blue and *rust* (Burnt Sienna) within that tone. The trees are also done with a simple flat tone. It is important to keep such areas uncomplicated to avoid a tedious, worked-over look.

Sepia and Cadmium Orange were used to form the ground patterns. The general form of the ruts is important, but it is not necessary to have too much detail. The grass was suggested with Chromium Oxide Green. Blues, orange, and sepia were applied in vertical washes

on cool and warm sides of shed—accented by sepia darks and orange (in roof).

Cart was kept simple by massing dark color. Rooster consists of two values of brown plus pure red.

The accents of fence wires, the crisp areas on roof, and the accents on the cart were painted in with opaque white rather than scratched out with a razor blade. Use white not to correct, but rather for accent. Finish by accenting with darks where appropriate.

In this sketch additional interest was created by grading the steeple as well as the lower portion of the church from dark down to light. This has the effect of suggesting additional dimension beyond that created by any perspective in the drawing.

On these pages the sketches gathered on the spot (in black and white in this case) suggest the eventual painting by their simplicity of statement. A subject as complicated as the dock scene on page 34 still keeps large areas massed so that they hold together as shapes. All the drawing is kept within these overall massed patterns.

Note the simplicity with which buildings are indicated to create pattern and atmosphere. This simplicity of statement can be carried into a finished painting with slight additional detail.

An excellent means of gathering material outdoors for future paintings, without worrying about control of washes, is to use the drawing pen or water color felt tip pen in combination with a limited number of colors, or simple washes using Lamp Black for value scales.

The painting below is an excellent example of the controlled use of an unrestricted palette. The application of contrasting and complementary color to the front of the building in the painting lends sparkle that adds great interest to the painting as a whole. This is possible because the additional color is basically kept within a value range that doesn't destroy the masses of light and shadow. Note the simplicity with which bushes and foreground to the left of the painting are treated.

Tuscany

The figure is quite often a necessary part of a landscape painting, and water color adapts extremely well to painting the human figure. In the examples on this page, the figure is the important element of the painting.

The sketch above shows one use of the sketching pen and ink with water color used to supply the color notes. All of the drawing, however, is held by the pen. This is an interesting technique. A useful adaptation is to draw with the ink into the wet paper, adding color when the surface is dry.

In this figure of a woman with market basket, a more finished painting, note the massing of feet and shadow, while detail and focus are concentrated in the upper portion of the figure.

Here is another approach utilizing loose massing of color. Figures are represented only as broad basic shapes; the focal point is the bright spot of balloons. The whole painting holds together extremely well. Try this loose massing of shapes, holding them together with simple drawing where necessary. Eliminate unimportant detail.

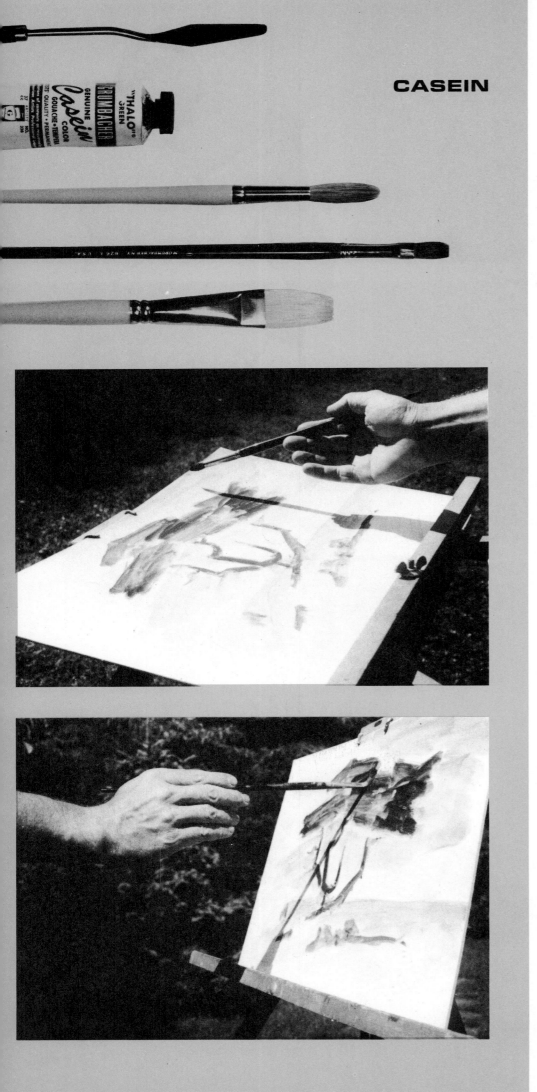

Casein has increased in popularity in recent years largely because of its great versatility. Casein is an aqueous medium which may be thinned sufficiently to be used as a wash. When used directly from the tube (just enough water to make it workable) or when mixed with white, casein is opaque and can be used as a gouache. Casein dries rapidly to a matte finish, and can be applied with water color brushes, oil brushes, (or with a painting knife for moderate impasto mounted water color paper, or canvas panels). Casein becomes increasingly waterproof as it dries.

Techniques of handling are similar to those you are familiar with for either water color or oil. Brushes must be washed thoroughly in soap and water after use. After the color (or the residue) hardens, the brush cannot be restored to its original state without difficulty.

Most artists work with casein as a tempera (gouache) (reducing the amount of water and mixing with white). The great covering power of the medium makes it excellent for use on tinted stock. By using casein as a tempera you can do a great deal of preliminary planning in pencil, and paint out what you don't want at the finish. You can also work directly over sketches.

In addition to its other properties casein serves as an excellent underpainting for oils. However, be sure to isolate such an under painting with a casein varnish before the application of oil colors otherwise the casein paint will absorb some of the oil and the painting will lack lustre. When used in the opaque technique, casein can be varnished and resembles an oil.

A complete range of artists' colors is available in casein. If you want to use the medium as water color or gouache, the brushes are the same as for water color. For slightly more impasto or oil techniques, oil brushes should be used.

The following demonstrations in casein were prepared by David Stone, who uses the medium for a great variety of exciting techniques.

A pencil sketch is made of the subject, as a first step to a casein painting. The trees, rocks, and hills in the background are arranged to form a balance within the picture area.

A pattern of lights, middle tones, and darks is painted in with a single color. These first steps establish a firm compositional foundation for the painting.

The tree limbs are rendered in colors used from the tube with very little water to keep their opaque quality. The areas in the sunlight have white mixed with the colors.

The last step in the painting is to paint in the lightest value in each area.

The red grid over the first sketch demonstrates one manner of composing a painting. Mountain peaks, valleys, trees, farms, etc., are moved around so that within each section of grid there is a general size relationship of various elements. This approach prevents any one area from becoming a spot lacking interest. The linear structure is roughly followed in the finish, and the organization is used as a basis for the painting without letting it dictate or inhibit technique. That is, once the elements have been organized, the painting should be finished with freedom and directness.

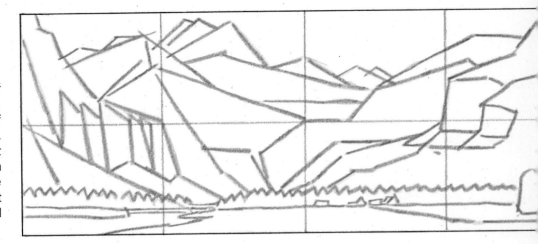

The sketch to the right shows the underpainting or tint preliminary to beginning the finished painting. The loose handling of color is kept within the pattern planned earlier. This pre-planning should never be so rigidly maintained that the painting becomes lifeless or stereotyped.

Painters interested in highly detailed work will find casein an excellent tool. The paint holds its opacity and brilliance even when thinned enough to work with a small brush for putting in fine detail.

On dark surfaces, casein can provide many unusual effects. This example illustrates the great covering power of the medium. A light-color pastel sketch is made on a colored surface and sprayed with fixative. Casein paint is applied thinly at first and then gradually built up in the light areas. The original black or toned surface should be allowed to show through to influence the color where needed and to become a part of the overall pattern of the painting.

For weekend in the country, a trip to a foreign land, or a walk in the back yard, a few pastels and a sketch pad can be a quick way to make color and value notes for future use.

POLYMER

One of the most recent and most interesting developments in material for the artist has been the introduction of polymer paints. Polymer plastic latex emulsion colors are extremely flexible, fast-drying, artists' quality water base paints which are insoluble in water once thoroughly dry. They can be handled as water colors, and the brilliance of the colors remain undiminished after application. They can also be used as impasto and built up to a much greater degree than casein without danger of chipping or cracking.

The copolymer medium (gloss or matte) can be used to thin the paint so that the cohesion of the paint will not be reduced. This is only important when working on less porous surfaces than canvas or paper. The mediums (which are the varnishes as well) change the reflective properties of the surface of the painting, and when used will give the painting a sheen. Polymer colors make an excellent underpainting for oil paints.

Polymers can be either transparent like water color or opaque like oils. Choice of brushes and other equipment should therefore be based on the effect you want to achieve—water color brushes for transparency, etc.

Wet-in-wet method.

The entire surface of the board or paper is soaked with clean water after the drawing has been penciled in. The paint is applied so that the color dissolves in part on the wet paper. The large areas are washed in first; successive areas depend on the degree of wetness or dryness desired for the statement involved. The basic painting should be completed before the paper has completely dried and details may then be added.

Pressed wood, cardboard, wood (sap free), cloth, plaster, acetate, raw canvas, and any non-oil surface can be primed with "Hyplar" prepared Gesso (acrylic polymer latex) to make an excellent painting surface. "Hyplar" Modeling Paste and Extender is the same base with a white marble dust extender, and can be used to build up impasto effects either directly or in mixture with the polymer colors.

There is a wide range of artists' colors available in "Hyplar."

Traditional water color method.
A wash of color is applied to each specific area on the dry surface to build up form and color throughout the painting. Textures can be applied using the dry brush technique once washes have dried. Wet-in-wet and traditional techniques may be combined in a painting.

"Hyplar" Gesso (ready-to-use painting ground) applied to pressed wood can also be used as a ground on any non-oil surface.

Modeling Paste-Extender can be mixed with color or applied as an underpainting for textures and impasto techniques.

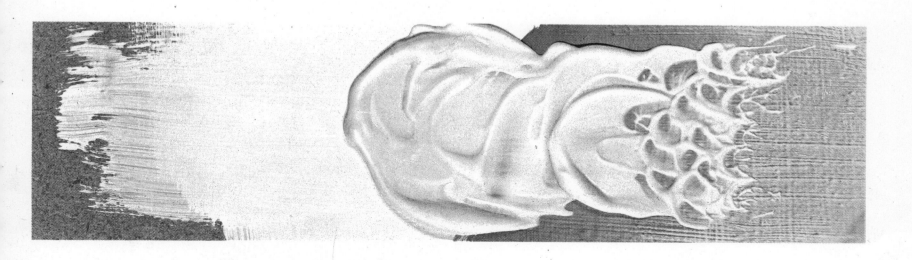

The Gesso may be used to develop an interesting painting surface by the way it is applied. The canvas or board was covered with the gesso using a stiff bristle brush. The sketch was made with a charcoal pencil and the paint scumbled over the surface using a dry brush technique, allowing the grain of the surface to show through.

In this impasto painting modeling paste-extender was mixed with the color, which was then applied with a palette knife. To accomplish this in oil paint would require days of drying time. The plastic paint dried thoroughly in a matter of hours.

On this page we see some of the preliminary steps for the painting that appears in full color on the following page. The subject was one calling for an impasto technique to express the roughness of the mountain landscape. Hyplar Modeling Paste was mixed with the paint to achieve a paste consistency which lends itself to modeling and different textures.

After much color balancing, the artist felt he needed more texture in the bark of the tree trunk. In this case he simply applied the Modeling Paste mixed with appropriate colors using a painting knife. The painting was finished by using thin washes of color over previously painted areas. The effect of glazing, as this is called, over the rough surface accentuated the texture and gave variety to the color.

U

Desk